BRITAIN IN OLD PH(

# AROUND

# POULTON-LE-FYLDE

*CATHERINE ROTHWELL*

ALAN SUTTON PUBLISHING LIMITED

Alan Sutton Publishing Limited
Phoenix Mill · Far Thrupp · Stroud
Gloucestershire · GL5 2BU

First published 1995

Copyright © Catherine Rothwell, 1995

Cover photographs: (front) golf club officials,
1924 (see p. 100); (back) Windsor Woolly
mannequins, 1930s.

British Library Cataloguing in Publication Data.
A catalogue record for this book is available from
the British Library.

ISBN 0-7509-1153-0

Typeset in 9/10 Sabon.
Typesetting and origination by
Alan Sutton Publishing Limited.
Printed in Great Britain by
Ebenezer Baylis, Worcester.

Dedicated to my friend the late Harry Hodgkinson,
born 1913, who 'in a long and varied life as
Intelligence Officer, oil company executive, expert on
Albanian affairs and distinguished travel writer'
(obituary in the *Independent*) never lost interest in his
roots around Poulton-le-Fylde.

# Contents

The Sportsman's Arms, Bull Street, owned by Queen's Brewery in 1900. Bearded J. Bamber, licensee, stands outside.

# Introduction

The area encompassed by *Around Poulton-le-Fylde in Old Photographs* comprises a number of ancient settlements at a time when influential families held sway: the Veales, patrons of the church at Bispham, where they held property; the Rigbys, with their mansion in Layton and fine house in Poulton; the Shireburns of Carleton Hall; and the powerful Fleetwood Heskeths, who controlled almost the whole length of the Lancashire coast. Weekly markets, annual fairs and festivals, with their additional privileges granted by charter, were all very much a part of medieval life, which persisted along with the regular use of cuckstool, stocks and whipping post. The great marshes of Carleton, Thornton and Rawcliffe had not then been drained.

By 1500 the 'Pulton', 'Polton' and 'Potton' of Saxon days had become 'Poolton', the town on the pool one mile from the River Wyre, with two ancient harbours. Its excellent nodal position ensured recovery after devastation by Danes and Normans, as no doubt did the presence of its church dedicated to the Saxon saint Cheadda, Bishop of Mercia. Possibly in existence as early as AD 689, this rare dedication is further proof of antiquity.

Eventually seven unpaved streets led to the market-place, with its moot hall and narrow entrance to the churchyard completely shut in by cottages. As so many people were brought from surrounding parishes for interment, the graveyard had to be extended several times; in 1595 there were 61 burials. An entry in the Churchwardens' Accounts reveals that one 'stranger', a visiting parson, was given a bottle of wine, but Parson Potter of Pilling actually fell asleep in the pulpit, his sermon ungiven. As the Jacobean pulpit is carved with the words 'Crie aloud; spare not; lift up thy voice like a trumpet,' this was not merely embarrassing to the St Chad's congregation, who quickly dispersed; it was ironic.

On market days stalls, booths and crowds filled the Square and spilled over into the churchyard. As Poulton's fairs were not granted by charter, itinerant pedlars forded the river and hawked their wares unhindered. These Mondays, when most people were about, were good opportunities to put felons in the stocks or administer whippings at the stone post. On May Bough Night young men climbed on to roofs to push branches of trees down chimneys, often damaging thatch in the process. A message was conveyed according to species: 'willow for a witch'; 'briar for a liar'; 'a plum tree in bloom, married soon'. Amid much raillery the biggest drunkard in town was elected mayor for a year and paraded aloft. Carriages were unusable in the mud and snow of winter so the gentry stayed in Poulton, visiting the newsroom at the Golden Ball Inn, one of the three coaching houses.

*Around Poulton-le-Fylde in Old Photographs* reveals some tough country characters, many living to a ripe old age. Margaret Barton, interviewed in 1887 when she became a centenarian, had 19 grandchildren, 32 great-grandchildren and 12 great-great-grandchildren. At 90 she had wielded a sickle during harvest time and was familiar with incidents in the battles of the Nile, Trafalgar and Waterloo, in which three of her relatives fought. The Jubilee of George III, and the accessions of George IV, William IV and Queen Victoria were fresh in her mind, but one topic roused her ire: 'With vigour she denounced the clergyman at Poulton's Parish Church who during alterations caused some sleepers in the churchyard to be removed at dead of night in order to realise his object.' Margaret Barton died in 1892 aged 105.

When Charles Dickens came to lecture in Blackpool on 21 April 1869 he was a sick man. To benefit from the fresh air he toured the Fylde, including Poulton. Many of the things he saw remained part of the scene as the years rolled on: bunches of dried sage hanging from the ceiling alongside a dripping pig; blue and white china; whitewashed cottages covered with red roses where cheese and butter were made. It was a time when characters abounded. One man dressed himself in Lincoln green and carried a longbow like Robin Hood. The tenant of Cockle Hall styled himself 'the only squire this side of Wyre'. 'Matey', a veteran of the Boer War who lived in the common lodging house in Potts Alley, pushed a pram full of old wheels which he would hang on hedgerows on his journey towards Layton. 'Pancake', an old lady, was plagued by naughty boys tying door knobs together and shouting after her. More recently, George Dalton, the last saddler, and Mr Clegg the clogger were remembered as a benevolent pair.

We learn about the past not only from plans, wills, tithe schedules, directories, ale-house recognisances, church registers, and hearth-tax returns in the Record Office, but from relics ploughed up. These have included coins, pewter, stone-age palstaves, an ice-age elk skeleton, swords and treasure trove hidden in thatch and walls. These pieces of jigsaw, when linked together and supplemented by old photographs, are indispensable in ascertaining the truth. 'Who cares?' mutters the cynic. Only the searcher knows the thrill. Salvaged from the shipwreck of time, one pure seed pearl of knowledge can suddenly illuminate that which could not previously be explained.

One such historian who enjoyed probing the past was W.T. Bulpit, curate at St Chad's. He had a theory supported by documents that Richard the Demon was present at an important gathering at Poulton Cross in the 13th century. All the chief men of the district assembled including Adam Banastre and the demon or deemster, an official of the Amounderness Hundred Court who gave legality to the meeting. What a photograph that would have made.

Catherine Rothwell<br>
Poulton-le-Fylde

## Section One

# POULTON-LE-FYLDE

*Church Street, 1902. W.H. Cooper ran the Bay Horse Inn (left). The Golden Ball, at right angles in Ball Street, was where tickets were booked for the theatre in the tithe-barn to see* Pisarro, the Spaniard *or* Maria Martin.

Stocks and whipping post, 1890s. The group including the market cross and fish slab (where market prices were settled) was referred to in the mid-19th century as 'the most complete example of its kind' and dates back to medieval days, when villages had by law to keep all these in good repair and to use them. The steps of the market cross are original, but the cobblestones in Market Square had been replaced by setts, because the former were so uncomfortable to walk upon that villagers called them 'petrified kidneys'. Other market crosses survive in the Fylde but Poulton is the only town to keep the cross on top of the plinth. On the right is Mr Lawrenson's printer's and stationer's shop; he later conducted his business from the tithe-barn, where he also sold antiques. Next door is one of the many fine town houses occupied by county families, but as time went on shop fronts were fitted to most premises.

One side of the Square was burned down in 1732, the fire being caused by a boy carrying an unprotected light. As all the buildings were then of wood and thatch, the west side of Market Square was razed. The funeral procession of important local man Geoffrey Hornby passing through to the church was showered with sparks and burning straw. At this time funerals were held at night, and as a mark of respect candles were burned in every window. A nationwide appeal was read in churches to repair the damage, estimated at £1,036.

The memorial brasses on the tombs of Geoffrey Hornby and his daughter inside the church of St Chad were removed to the wall when the chancel floor was raised in 1883.

Wheatsheaf Street, 18th century. On the left at no. 16 lived Richard and Samuel Lomas, who maintained the clock of St Chad's Church. 'Sam Lomas, Poolton' appears on the faces of their now valuable grandfather clocks. Opposite are the tall, three-storey Georgian houses presently under a preservation order, as is the Lomases' house.

Leading to the port of Poulton, 18th-century Breck Street was lined with thatched cottages. It was one of seven streets which, according to the Revd William Thornber's book (see p. 10), were 'unpaved, the inhabitants holding connection with each other's dwelling by stepping stones'.

The Revd William Thornber when he was minister at St John's Church, Blackpool. Son of Giles Thornber, who became a country magistrate, he was born in Breck Street at the end adjoining Ball Street. William's book, *Historic Description of Blackpool and Neighbourhood*, was printed in 1837. From this we learn much about Poulton's history. He remembered the bells of St Chad ringing out for victory at Waterloo. 'Our house at Poulton was decorated with tiles around the fireplace made by J. Sadler. Old Simpson, watch maker, always fitted a painted piece of paper into the case. Many of these watch-papers, beautifully worked, were put in the turnip watches. . . . The town's well at the top of the Green is opposite Hornby's house; old Mr Dixon has water brought every morning from the well at High Cross.' He described the many customs: the pace-egging songs at Easter; the 'ignagning' or jolly-ladding, so boisterous that villagers were glad to pay and be rid of the young men who burst into homes late at night. William lived until 1885, but his last years, troubled by mental illness, were most unhappy.

'Ralph Robinson *me fecit* [made me] 1741' is inscribed on the cracked bell preserved at St John's Roman Catholic church, and presently used to grace flower festivals. A wonderful 16th-century vestment is also a treasure. As the Catholics at Singleton could not get their licence renewed, they came to Poulton in 1813. One 5 November, desirous of a grand bonfire, the villagers of Singleton went round begging for peat, but the RC priest refused. They were so incensed that the priest was turned out of house and church. The original church, built near Moorland Road, has become the church hall. In 1911 Tom Beesley of Skippool laid the foundation stone of a new church, which opened in the time of Canon Vaughan.

'Windsor Registered Water Woollies', 1932. The little boy is Neville Windsor, third generation in the family business started by Benjamin Windsor (who was born in 1872). While employed as a coachman to Dr Jukes at Longridge, Benjamin met his future wife Elizabeth – who had already won a national embroidery competition. To please friends they both knitted socks, shawls and babies' wear. With their two sons Albert and William, who also learned the skill, they embarked upon a great enterprise in 1905. Such was the quality of their work that they received more and more orders and opened a shop in Colne. All the girls whom they employed were trained to their high standards of craftsmanship. William walked up to 20 miles a day taking orders. As their fame spread, ladies travelled into Colne to patronise their shop, the interior of which Benjamin had constructed from 16th-century beams. In 1926 the trade name Windsor was registered, and in the same year B. Windsor and Sons Ltd was incorporated, with Albert and William, now in their twenties, appointed directors. The Poulton-le-Fylde factory, later known as Castle Works, was built that same year.

The Railway and Station Hotel was run by Samuel Castle when this photograph was taken, c. 1900. Situated on the corner of Breck Street across from the present Station Road, it was one of the many inns and hotels that Poulton, in its heyday as 'Metropolis of the Fylde', could fill to capacity. From the 18th-century list of Lancashire fixed and moveable fairs we find that the town annually held three, in February, April and November. On weekly market days, or 'flesh days' before Christmas, and at horse and cattle sales, farmers and wives came to Poulton from miles around.

Across the road from the Railway and Station Hotel was the Royal Oak, where every June sheep shearing took place by the old Railway Crossings. This was Poulton's Wool Day, when gigs, lorries and carts brought in masses of fleeces which were auctioned on the spot. There was a dye house in this area, which coloured the waters of the pond where the ducking stool was kept, until the railway came in 1840 and this area was culverted.

Poulton had a tannery and skin house at Low Cross, a rope works in Sandy Lane, and Mr Harrison kept the inmates of the workhouse in Queen's Square busy weaving sailcloth (harden) for the shipping at Skippool. This trade also needed lots of handmade nails until they were supplanted by cheaper, machine-made nails from the Midlands in 1846. Indeed the number of hotels indicates the importance and distinction the town enjoyed in those commercially busy days.

The presence of two telegram boys seated on the old fish slab indicates the post office behind, *c.* 1870. The post office moved to the Breck in 1934 when Mr Kirkham's house was pulled down, but the residents did not like this and it moved back into Market Square. The town house in front of the stocks later became a bank, but was once the Rigby family residence; their stone coat of arms dated 1697 was above the door. This now lies at the foot of the church tower in front of an 18th-century font (see p. 29). The postmaster at the time of demolition saved fragments of stained-glass windows from the Rigby mansion. The whipping post in the foreground had years before lost the iron manacles to which malefactors were chained. Whipping took place at the rogues' post on market days when most people were around. The culprit had details of his offence written in large letters on a paper fixed to his head. Records show that both stocks and whipping post were frequently repaired. On the ancient steps of the market cross have stood Charles Dickens and Keir Hardie, not to mention the bellman who read out notices from this vantage point.

Dudley Hall in Bull Street, *c.* 1900. This was supposedly used by Henry VII's extortioners Empsom and Dudley, notorious for their method of extracting taxes by 'Morton's Fork', a two-pronged approach which none could escape. This thatched cottage, possibly 400 years old, and the last to go in Poulton, was lived in by the Swarbrick family, well known for their tasty parched peas. Before it was demolished in 1961 the last occupant did not want to leave, but the site was earmarked for the new Lancashire Library. At some time Bull Street became Blackpool Old Road. When the Black Bull Inn was still flourishing in the 1920s there were a number of fine houses and businesses along Bull Street: John Birch, joiner and wheelwright; Mr Thompson, horticulturist; Lloyd's glass works; G. Carter's corn mill; Sir William Hodgson's house The Sycamores; and a row of terraced cottages including the Old England Café, originally the Sportman's Arms. At the top of Bull Street as it joined the Square was the longest-established ironmonger's shop in the Fylde, owned by E. Richards and Son who made nails by hand.

W. Knight's Bay Horse Inn (left), c. 1892. It faced what was known as The Twenty Steps, a towering house, backing as so many did on to the churchyard of St Chad. This degenerated into a lodging house but must have been grand at one time. Note the twenty-paned Queen Anne bow window (right) with its slender glazing bars. These houses were pulled down in 1911 and a strong stone retaining wall built around the churchyard. The Bay Horse became the town hall. Pratt's Motor Spirit was sold next door at the cycle and repair shop, outside which was the favourite stamping ground of the knife and scissors sharpener who pushed his grinding machine around the streets.

Beyond the wall-mounted bracket lamp is the 18th-century Golden Ball Hotel, where men of consequence gathered in the newsroom. It was here that Giles Thornber learned of the victories at Waterloo and the Battle of the Nile. Cattle were driven along Church Street for sale in the market-place until 1897, when the town became so congested that an auction mart with pens was set up behind the Golden Ball. In the reign of Queen Anne the collector of customs lived in this area. He received a salary of £30 a year, but by 1840 Stephen Burridge, who then held the post, moved to Fleetwood, was promoted in salary and the new port was declared 'open to all the world'.

Grace Poole, here photographed in Herbert Wilde's studio, Blackpool, in about 1880, was in service in Poulton. Old directories show that houses in Lockwood Avenue, Breck Street, Market Place and Tithebarn Street had maids, cooks, housekeepers and coachmen; servants' wages were low and hours long. Possibly a relation of the Misses Margaret and Jenny Poole who lived at this time on the Breck, Grace hailed from Hambleton. Her family has been traced back to the early 17th century. Girls' names Grace and Ann, and boys' names John, James and Robert recur frequently in the family.

This type of lamp, one of the last of its kind remaining locally when it was photographed in 1960, was quite common in the late 19th century. Indeed, there were a number in St Chad's churchyard and in Market Square, and also in the driveways of Edwardian villas such as this one on Breck Road next to the civic centre. Of similar wrought-iron construction but with a differently shaped globe is the century-old one outside the Shard Bridge Hotel, which was to warn the ferryman, and others on the River Wyre at night, not to proceed further.

In the 1890s, when this photograph was taken, the Tennis Club met at Higher Longfield off Tithebarn Street, the area where in 1809 the Elders of the Congregational Chapel bought 480 square yards of land for £24 on which to build their chapel.

Fylde Cricket Club, 1876. In 1946 a local man, T.B. Silcock, gave to the National Playing Fields Association a 4-acre field on Moorland Road that was to be at the disposal of the Cricket Club.

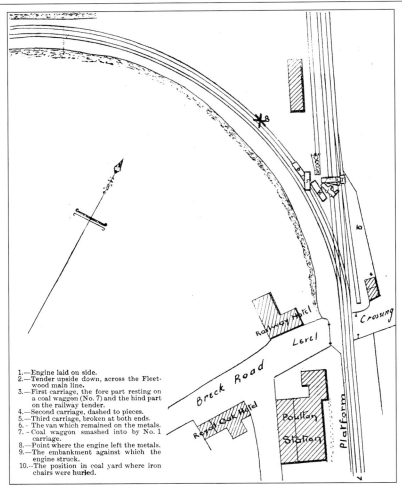

1.—Engine laid on side.
2.—Tender upside down, across the Fleet-
    wood main line.
3.—First carriage, the fore part resting on
    a coal waggon (No. 7) and the hind part
    on the railway tender.
4.—Second carriage, dashed to pieces.
5.—Third carriage, broken at both ends.
6. - The van which remained on the metals.
7. - Coal waggon smashed into by No. 1
    carriage.
8.—Point where the engine left the metals.
9.—The embankment against which the
    engine struck.
10.--The position in coal yard where iron
    chairs were hurled.

The map from *Plan with views of the Railway Disaster at Poulton*, price 1*d*, issued on
Monday 3 July 1893. Late on a Saturday night, with darkness adding to the horror, the
engine driver Cornelius Ridgway and two passengers were killed and many more
seriously injured. An inquest was held at the Royal Oak Hotel 'where the bodies were
laid out in a room in the basement and a gruesome spectacle they presented, traces of
blood which flowed from terrible wounds being distinctly visible on the floor'. Mr
Gilbertson, District Coroner, presided with a jury composed of three vicars and eleven
well-known Poultonians, including Bowman, Lawrenson, Grime and Catterall, names
which had been on the committee responsible for Queen Victoria's Jubilee celebrations.

The loop of line at the bottom of the Breck had for years been regarded with
suspicion. Walter Chamberlain, travelling nearest to the engine and seated next to Healy
and Marsh, both of whom were killed, described terrific jolts, stunning shocks and his
frenzied efforts to climb on to the splintered roof amidst steam and gas. Captain
Ibbitson, the chairman of the inquiry, revealed the hazardous nature of Poulton Curve
in his report, and the railway company was charged with culpable negligence.

The first carriage in the railway disaster of 3 July 1893. The Railway and Station Hotel opposite was turned into a temporary hospital. Using bedding and table linen as wound dressings, Mr W.H. Heaton, aided by his wife, attempted to succour 32 injured passengers.

Breck station on the Preston and Wyre Railway line, c. 1890, near where a Roman coin was found in 1852. After the accident the station was moved to the top of Breck Road. This new station had one of the longest platforms in the country and traffic was controlled by a staff of twenty-nine.

Robert Poole Roe, *c.* 1875. Born 9 April 1853, he moved from Liverpool to Poulton or Rawcliffe and was a member of Poulton Brass Band, which was formed on 25 September 1875. In 1925 four of the original members were still alive: Ralph Parr, who joined when he was 12, T. Bradley, T. Fairclough and N. James. The band played on every major occasion, attending not only Poulton Club Day but all the other galas around Poulton. They practised at the Thatched House Inn in the 19th century, but by the 1960s were using Mr Lloyd's glass works for meetings.

Poulton had a number of dame schools as the town prospered. Ada Constance Agnes Barnes, photographed at Ash Martin's Studio in Fleetwood in about 1907, assisted at Kate Margaret Valiant's Academy. Miss Valiant, who lived in Market Place, purchased the premises from Elizabeth Rogers in the 1880s but had previously taught at the RC school on the Breck. At that time Elizabeth Tebay was in charge of the National School in Sheaf Street, the Misses Clara and Mary Cryer ran Breck Villas, and Miss Edith Rogerson Warwick House in Ball Street. By the 1930s, apart from the High School (boarding and kindergarten) run by Miss E. Atkin and Miss E. Gee, which had been Westbourne House, state education catered for most children.

The steps of this ancient cross may be older than those of the market cross. The Revd W.T. Bulpit, curate at St Chad's Church, reported in 1871 that the plate (gnomon) of the octagonal sundial shaft had been stolen. He found no trace at that time of Breck Cross, an ancient town boundary marker at the corner of Little Poulton Lane.

A class at the National School, Sheaf Street, with their pupil teacher in the centre, c. 1892. In December 1909, three days before Christmas, snow was so deep that 128 children were absent and the pitiful remainder were sent home by the headmaster, concerned about their wet state.

This archway was built by Judge Edward Abbot Parry in 1897 to mark Queen Victoria's Diamond Jubilee. The circuit judge lived at 46 Breck Road, and when his gracious house was eventually acquired as part of Poulton College of Education in 1959 it was decided that the archway must be demolished. The farm attached to the Jubilee arch was also pulled down and a new entrance made in readiness for the opening of the College. On 4 January 1988, after further expensive and lengthy refurbishing, the building opened as the new Wyre Civic Centre.

Used as the principal's residence in the days of the College of Education, Judge Parry's house is now almost 200 years old. One wing of the main building was completed in the 1930s as the Cross Convalescent Home for cotton spinners (see p. 67). The judge liked to do some of his own shopping and went to Leadbetter's Fleetwood fish shop for lobsters. He wrote some charming books for children that were based on Fylde scenes; in *Butterscotia* he describes the ferry boats at Fleetwood.

A Poulton Urban District survey in 1908 revealed that the width of Church Street was little over 20 ft. Passing the group of children is a milk float and a new-fangled motor car, with the registration number FR 173, and complete with chauffeur, waits outside the grocer's shop. Narrow Chapel Street was similarly surveyed.

The junction of Breck Road near Moorland Road, *c.* 1900. On the left is Breck Lodge, where James Sykes lived. He is listed in Slater's 1882 Directory together with 81 other 'Gentry and Clergy'. Massey's Burnley Ales were popular at the Station Hotel (right). Breck Lodge is now a nursing home for the elderly.

Church Street, 1917. Next to the three-storey building of Elliott's, tailors and outfitters, is Long's baker's shop and dining rooms. Beyond is the Bay Horse and the present-day entrance to Teanlowe shopping centre. In the centre is yet another inn, the King's Head, which was later to become a bank.

Fleetwood Docks, 1880s. On the left is the *Livorno* and in the centre a masted ship carrying timber from the Baltic for Riley's saw mills. Goods were brought from abroad to the port of Fleetwood for Poulton merchants, such as Mr Parkinson, miller, one of whose shipments of flour was lost on the high seas.

Wagonettes outside the Bull Inn were a familiar sight in about 1900 and, before the Preston and Wyre Railway opened, the arrival of the stage coach was the delight of small boys. Drawn by four horses, it approached via Breck Street, carrying passengers and the mail. If snow delayed its progress the postboy would ride into town on horseback. The Black Bull Inn was a posting house and meeting place for the trustees of Baines's Grammar School, one of three schools endowed by James Baines, a wealthy woollen chapman who died in 1717. In 1828 his trustees rebuilt the school. It was they who decided whether a child should be educated there and made into a good apprentice.

'March 21st 1837 Rent Day held at James Taylor's Bull Inn, an excellent dinner served. Trustees Messrs Thornber, Dickson, Wilson and Hall present. Mr Kemp, Peter Hesketh's steward, dined with us. He wanted to treat for the land the railway takes up at Puddle House Estate.' (Hornby Porter's diary.) The rents from Puddle House farm helped to maintain the school. It is thought that James Baines's house, from where he conducted business, was situated next door to the Bull, where the bank and grocer appear on this photograph.

Poulton Savings Bank, dating from 1839, is presently occupied by Butson's, estate agents, at the Ball Street corner of Vicarage Road. It was a useful building for early council meetings, which later progressed to the masonic hall and town hall when the council purchased the Bay Horse Inn.

The old brick croft from William Raby's brick and tile manufacturer, Station Road, was discovered at 9 Fylde Road in 1974. The chimney had been demolished long ago but bricks still turn up in gardens. William was listed as brickmaker in 1889, when William Ellison was his manager.

The Methodist church at the corner of Chapel Street and Higher Green, 1904. It was demolished in 1965 and a new church was built in Queensway. The Methodist pioneers date from 1819 but they were given a rough reception in Poulton. Thomason's grocer's shop is on the right.

The town turns out for Queen Victoria's Golden Jubilee in 1887, having provided the tall lamp on the right to mark the occasion. Poulton Brass Band are in the centre circle. At the end of the Square, where the moot hall was situated in Saxon times, is the Cyclists' Rest, a temperance inn. Jubilee Terrace dates from this year.

A horse sale, *c.* 1903. Elliotts, tailors and outfitters, have moved to premises next to the bank, previously the Cyclists' Rest. From time immemorial the Fylde was renowned for horses and bloodstock (Rossall/Roshale means horse pasture). These sales were famous, as were those at Garstang. The boys mingling with the men may well be hoping for 'horse jobs', which entailed leading a horse to its new home or possibly taking a horse to the smithy and back, which could take half a day.

Horses were indispensable to the economy, and were needed for pulling carts, floats, gigs, muck spreading, ploughing, general jobs on the farm and carting around town. Stallions were regularly taken to the mews area behind the Ship Inn and the Golden Ball by prior arrangement, so that mares could be served. Woe betide the boy who galloped or attempted to ride these valuable beasts when such arrangements were in hand. Ponies were stabled at The Ship for drawing light carts or 'sulkies' in the trotting races held near the Wyreside Hotel at Skippool, and there was horse racing at Shard in the early 19th century. Mr Sykes of Breck Lodge was well known for his hackney horses, and Mr Comptsy for his Breck Stud of shire horses.

THE VICARAGE          POULTON

The Vicarage in Vicarage Lane (now Road), 1898. This was built by public subscription in about 1835 after the demolition of an ancient thatched, cruck cottage used by vicar Peter Whyte, who lived to the age of ninety. Vicar Harrison insisted on flagged floors and no old-fashioned casement windows at his vicarage in the 17th century.

Willows grew in profusion in the extensive grounds. An 18th-century font found there now reposes at the foot of the church tower. Garden parties were held on the lawns in front of this large house, the ladies' egg and spoon race being a feature. In the 1860s the Rev. John Hull employed a governess, coachman and servants, whereas in 1851 there were five servants and a footman. When this house was in turn pulled down and a new vicarage built higher up the road, the site was used for tennis courts in the Jean Stansfield Memorial Park. The low, cobbled wall of 'duck stones' from the seashore was typical of many in the Fylde, but most have now been swept away.

An old gentleman and child pause for the street photographer, unaware of a moment in history, and of how different the pace of life would be 100 years on.

In the late 19th century Higher Green retained many of its thatched cottages. The road in this ancient quarter led to Lower Green, where May Day celebrations took place. There was maypole dancing, the strewing of flowers, the election of a king and queen at the ancient 'shutting of marl' ceremony, and home-brewed ale was handed to passers-by.

This Queen Anne window in the old tithe-barn, photographed in 1960, had been removed from the court house in Queen's Square, when it was being refurbished as a library in the 1930s. Until well into the 1890s county court meetings had been held in the court house every four weeks under Judge William Hulton.

An important wedding, 1900. The narrow entrance to St Chad's Church was still hemmed in by tall buildings at this time. On the left is the bank; on the far right is the county police building, while Whittons' shop frontage has taken possession of one of Poulton's grand town houses. A century before this, because roads were virtually impassable, the titled and the wealthy business people spent the winter season in Poulton.

Before Marton, Thornton and Fleetwood had their own parish churches, the long journey for weddings, baptisms and funerals had to be made to Poulton. On 13 May 1656 seven couples were married. At that time the vicar and five churchwardens were members of the group of 24 sworn men who had the governance of the town.

In Market Place in 1910 lived Richard Parkinson, saddler; John Roe, ironmonger and iron merchant; William Bunn, confectioner; Charles Butler, butcher; Joseph Roe, tailor; and William Ball, painter and plumber.

Market Place, 1887. In honour of Queen Victoria's 50th year on the throne, Poulton residents erected a tall gas lamp near the market cross and leading men voted for a photograph to mark the occasion. George III was also honoured in Poulton in the 50th year of his reign.

County families – the Veales, Fleetwoods and Heskeths – are remembered by the lozenge-shaped hatchments in the Georgian gallery of St Chad. Among them is the royal coat of arms, recently cleaned. When a monarch died this record had to be altered, so it was taken to Great Eccleston when George III died. The job cost the churchwardens £8.

On 19 July 1821 the Coronation of George IV was celebrated by giving a hearty meal in Market Place to the children, old men and women of Poulton. The king's health was drunk amid cheers, and there was good roast beef and bread.

Poulton's medieval relics, especially the stocks, were increasingly damaged – as here in th 1920s – as more traffic passed through Market Place. Stocks date from Edward III's reign and were usually placed near the church, opposite the principal inn. Fish stones varied in shape from town to town; some, for example those at Kirkham, were circular.

The county police building, 1920s. Although the ground floor remained unchanged, a second storey was added in recent time, to the original 1890s premises.

The medieval tithe-barn in process of demolition, *c.* 1976. Services were held in the tithe-barn when the church was being rebuilt in 1751, and later Blackpool visitors arrived in bathing vans to see plays performed here. In the late 1960s A. Riding, painter and decorator, and Ogdens, oxyacetylene welders, had premises in the barn.

Inventor John Leyland Birley's locomotive, 1893. The influential Kirkham mill owners settled a branch of the family in Poulton in the 18th century. John Birley, along with John Bird and Richard Tennant, organised the building of the gallery at St Chad's in 1751, disposing of pews to recoup building costs. John Birley had a double pew for his large family.

Dr James Anderson of Glenelg, Breck in Market Square, *c.* 1890. He is wearing silk top hat and frock coat, and is playfully talking to a barefoot youngster near the police station. Along with Dr Winn he attended the wounded after the railway accident at Poulton Curve.

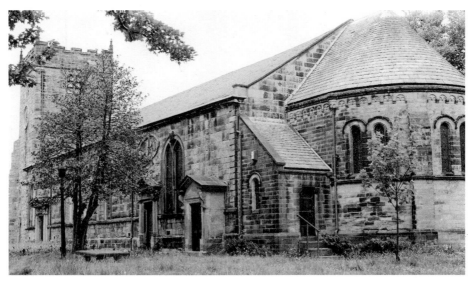

A semicircular apse was added to St Chad's by the Revd Thomas Clarke in 1868. More alterations were made in 1883, when the organ was removed from the west gallery and choir stalls were placed in the chancel; 1955 saw the addition of a central aisle.

Queen's Square, August 1906. On the left are Parkinson's grocer's shop and café, the latter run by Miss Anne Balderstone. The initials of the first Mr Parkinson (RAP) were in the roof design. This mews area led to Dick Hodgson's small jam factory. Mr McMullen baked bread with flour from the corn mill in Chapel Street.

Part of the classical frieze from above Parkinson's shop in Queen's Square, 1920. Originally terracotta, it was later painted blue. Placed there by the first Mr Parkinson of Parkinson Tomlinson's corn mill, it represented the harvesting of cereals and is over 100 years old.

An entry for Poulton Club Day, later known as Festival or Gala, stands outside Hugh Simmons, blacksmiths, 1900. Hugh's floats were most ambitious, carrying anvil, hammers, lots of horseshoes and even a horse. The business dated from 1890 and continued until the 1950s.

Outside the police station in Market Square, this group of ex-servicemen wearing their war decorations await Edward, Prince of Wales's inspection in 1927. On the second row, extreme right, the second and third men from the end are Arthur Gleave, wearing a trilby, and Bert Darlington, who was a baker and confectioner.

A mystery photograph from an 1890s glass plate negative. What was this boiler doing in Queen's Square? It may have been supplied by W.L. Holland of Preston, 'Engineers, Mills and Works Furnishers, Brassfounders'. A hoist in the background is probably that of Queen's Brewery, where Catterall and Swarbrick brewed ale and porter.

Bradshaw and Company, asphalters, with their tar boilers and workmen making Beach Road (previously Cemetery Lane) in Fleetwood, 1927. They had contracts all over the Fylde at that time as new roads to the coast were under construction. Garstang Road, Poulton was part of the town's 'five year plan' in the 1930s.

'Vortex' was the pseudonym of W. Haslam, who wrote a weekly article in the *Blackpool Gazette* for many years on matters concerning Poulton. His subjects ranged widely, from old customs to buildings, rates and sewerage. He also served on the Poulton Urban District Council (see p. 63), being deputy chairman in April 1937 when Councillor R.P. Tomlinson was invested with the chain of office, having been elected for the sixth time.

Mr Haslam had the fortunes of Poulton and the surrounding villages very much at heart, and among many projects worked hard to create a reading room, lecture hall and library in the old institute on the corner of Hardhorn Road, which was originally the court house.

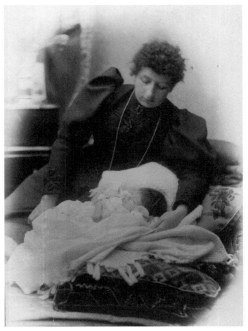

This Poulton lady and her baby were callers at Mrs Maxwell's Lighthouse Studio in the 1880s, when both Fleetwood and Poulton were prospering. Photographers or 'likeness takers' were in the ascendancy. Some were chemists, but for a lady to set up in this kind of business, which involved dangerous chemicals, was unusual. Messrs Ash Martin and Nickson covered the Fleetwood town scenes but Mrs Maxwell was pronounced 'very good with children'. In Poulton, J. Maynard Tomlinson and Mr Lord were professional photographers from the 1890s onwards, specialising in buildings, changing scenes in the countryside and important events.

The Chrysanthemum Show committee in 1930 reveals many old Poulton family names. Not among them, but a great helper at all the flower shows which had flourished since the 19th century, was Mr James Threlfall. One year, there was an outcry voiced by 'Vortex' in the *Blackpool Gazette* against dyed chrysanthemums, which to him were anathema. The annual general meeting was held in Mrs Huddlestone's café and, most appropriately, they met in the office of Mr H.A.E. Plant (born 1864), whose hobbies included growing roses and carving ivory.

Standing, left to right: P. Wilkinson, Billy Baines, J. Ashton, T. Sanderson, Mr Smalley, Henry Hodgson, -?-, -?-, -?-, -?-, -?-, Robert Simmons, Mr Holland, Robert Balderstone. Front row: Mr Coupe, Mr Potter, the Revd W.S. Mellor (vicar of St Chad's), small boy, Mr and Mrs Sharple of The Uplands, Mr Warbrick (the Congregational minister), Mr George Minshull, -?-, -?-.

At least four of these men were gardeners by trade, including George Minshull, at The Manor on Moorland Road, and Robert Balderstone, a successful market gardener.

The first managers of Hodgson Senior School, 13 April 1932. Front row, left to right: G. Woodhouse, Miss Hodgson, Mrs Potts, A.L. Poole (County Councillor and Chairman), William Hodgson, H.A.E. Plant, the Revd T.H. Watson. Back row: R.P. Tomlinson, T.C. Weston, J.P. Dobson, H. Stonestreet, W. Sanderson, R. Parkinson, J.A. Farrand (Headmaster), the Revd W. S. Mellor.

A group of Hodgson School staff and pupils photographed outside the front entrance of the school, 1935. Headmaster J.A. Farrand is in the centre of the middle row, and among the girls at the back are Gwen Yates, Edith Walsh and Hilda Stone.

Well-known old Poultonians in 1910: the Misses Viener with brother Harry, who was a chaplain in the Royal Flying Corps. They lived in a fine Georgian house in Queen's Square next to the old court house, where sessions were held from 1770. Miss Long, seen on p. 56, was their cook and housekeeper. Edith (right), popularly known as 'Polly' Viener, who had a jeweller's shop in Blackpool, taught languages at night school and was the Guide mistress. Ethel (left), referred to herself as Scout master, and was in charge of Cubs and Scouts.

Nowadays two shop fronts project over what once were the two lawns of the Vieners' house. It was a regular 'good turn' for the scout troop to march to the Viener residence and pick off all the daisies growing on these lawns. The Vieners were also interested in supporting the Royal National Lifeboat Institution. By 1934 their White House was having shop fronts inserted, but the recessed Georgian door can still be seen.

Professor J.H. Moore, Punch and Judy and ventriloquist entertainer, who performed on Blackpool sands in the 1920s, was also available at galas and parties in Poulton and the Fylde villages. One Poulton apprentice, assisted by Baines's Charity, was trained in 'the mysteries of Punch and Judy' in about 1828 by a Mr Scott.

Queen's Square in the snows of 1940, when the War Memorial was situated in its original place. Owing to traffic problems in later years it was moved to Market Square. The Stocks Café was at one time the residence of Ernest George Best Starkie, Medical Officer of Health, and some ten years ago stacks of medical records relating to Poulton and the Fylde were found in a room when these old premises were being altered.

On the opposite corner was the institute, once the county court, attached to the Misses Vieners' house. Among visiting lawyers was a clever advocate from Bolton known locally as 'Fat Duck', though he was small in stature. John Whiteside was high bailiff and John Pattinson registrar in 1882.

The crew of the suction pump dredger named *Poulton* in honour of the town, 1906. John R. Wright, second from left at the front, was mate but later became skipper. A twin-screwed vessel built at Paisley in 1899, the *Poulton* had a dredging capacity of 1,500 cubic yards per hour.

Chapel Street, looking towards the Ship Inn (which by 1929 was the Conservative Club), 1899. The cart is almost level with the Thatched House Inn adjoining St Chad's church yard. Anyone caught here 'Sabbath breaking' in the 18th century was marched into church by the beadle, and the innkeeper was fined.

This impressive scene in Market Square was when inhabitants assembled to sing 'God Save the King', before the service at the parish church of St Chad on 12 May 1937. The occasion marked the Coronation of King George VI and Queen Elizabeth. Near the lamp in the foreground stand the Poulton Urban District Council officials, among them (wearing the chain of office) the chairman of the council, Councillor R. Parkinson Tomlinson, who delivered an address of loyalty. On the far right is the masonic hall, where at one time the council held its meetings. There are representatives from the various associations and many schoolchildren. Reluctantly, the council had to abandon a scheme for souvenir handkerchiefs to mark the occasion but an allowance of 1s per schoolchild had been voted by the county council to be spent on coronation celebrations. Employees of Poulton Urban District Council were granted a holiday with pay. Flags, bunting and a 'God Save the King' banner embellished the ancient square on this special occasion.

The weeks leading up to Christmas were very busy with a thronged Market Place for 'T' Fither Sale' (feather). Thousands of birds – geese, turkey, cockerels, ducks – were brought for sale along with 'baby beef' the week before Christmas. 'Vortex' reported on 28 lb turkeys being sold, a size which only the farm and hotel ovens could cope with.

Poulton Gala, 1929. The Square is crowded as the procession makes its way through towards Higher and Lower Green. To the annoyance of some townspeople this traditional route is no longer allowed. Present-day processions held during the first week in June wend their way to Cottam Hall playing fields. Horses were always a great feature and hours were spent in grooming their coats, plaiting manes, burnishing hooves and polishing horse brasses, of which some Poulton men had large collections. Rosettes and ribbons decorated the floats and a patriotic theme prevailed – Britannia is in the leading cart. Morris dancers in Poulton were trained by George Bibby, but troupes from Carleton, Thornton, Fleetwood and Singleton also joined in, as did the brass bands culled from around Poulton.

On Club Days at the turn of the century the morris dancers went as far as the River Wyre Hotel where the girls were refreshed with glasses of lemonade. Morris dancing goes back to the days of the Long Morris, performed by strong men who pulled the rush cart to St Chad's when the church floor was strewn with rushes, which were renewed twice a year. The last occasion was in 1813.

All the pupils attending Westbourne House School, with Headmistress Miss Margaret Wilson in the centre, 1921. The school was situated at the corner of Elletson Street and Lockwood Avenue, premises which are now used as education offices. At the rear were large, beautifully kept lawns used for plays and performances of scenes from Shakespeare.

Part of this school for girls, well remembered for its high academic tradition, was a well-equipped gymnasium, Swedish drill then being popular. There was also a kindergarten class. Concerts were a feature at each prize-giving, which commenced with the school song 'Land of Our Birth', followed by dances, and violin and piano solos given by the pupils. Scenes from *Twelfth Night* were performed on 2 April 1928, when the Revd W.S. Mellor presented the prizes and certificates.

Poulton Amateur Dramatic Society's performance of *The Barretts of Wimpole Street* in the Church Hall, Vicarage Road, *c.* 1934. Mr and Mrs Paterson, Cyril Palanque, Keith Bamber, Harry and Bill Longworth and Arthur Heywood were in the cast.

The same amateur dramatic group presented *Cupid Rampant* in a subsequent year, 1930s. On the left, hands in pockets, is William Yates.

A Sheaf Street School class, 1926. Many of the names have been remembered by an old inhabitant. Back row, left to right: Johnnie Whitaker, Albert Mocket, Abey Turner, -?-, -?-, -?-, Clifford Wood, -?-, ? Fisher, Freddie Longworth. Second row: Jack Penswick, Bill Bamber, Elsie Bamber, Hilda Stone, Laura Ensery, Grace Harmer, -?-, -?-, Dorothy Walsh, Maggie Butler, Cathy Thompson, Dickie Bailey, Fred Swarbrick, -?-. Third row: Emily Webster, Lily Graham, Elsie Bullock, Jennie Fisher, Nora Dickinson, Muriel Cowell, Mary Howard, Nancy Meredith. Front row: Sammy Jenkins, Billy Yates, Nellie Billington, Eileen Tebay, Mary Blakey, Fred Carter, Ernie Broadhurst.

At this time the population of Poulton-le-Fylde was 2,800, and the township comprised 914 acres with a rateable value of £44,399. J.K. Thomas was the Medical Officer of Health.

Mrs Norah Haslam crowns Joyce Geldart Poulton Festival Queen of 1934. This annual festival or club day commenced over a century ago as a men-only procession, with the flaunting of silk banners of their lodges and societies, but grew in popularity until all the family joined in.

A garden party held at Fylde Cricket Club, 1960s. Traditionally there was always a home-made jam, cake and wine stall. Old residents, who called Christmas 'Kesmus', would make up to 20 Christmas puddings for the next year. Rich cakes and large jars of jam and mincemeat were set aside for family and events such as this.

Opening of the Jean Stansfield Memorial Park, June 1926 (see p. 53). In the centre is bearded Mr Potts, Chairman of the Urban District Council. Mrs 'Queenie' Stansfield, Mr S.F. Stansfield (holding coat) and Mr R.P. Tomlinson are also in the group as three rousing cheers are called for.

Form III M, Baines Grammar School, 1931. The boys on the back row are, left to right, Billington, Peter Bee, Makin, Harrison, Winder, Tattersall and Laski. Yates, Lang and Friar are also in the group. Mr Hood was form master.

Miss Anderson with the kindergarten class of Westbourne House School, 1930. Brian Haslam is the boy on the extreme right. Joyce Allen and Freda Mellor (the vicar of St Chad's daughter) are also in the picture.

The Dainty Dots were trained by Marie Felton (centre) in 1932. From the left they are Edie Simmonds, Renee Leeming, Gwennie Yates, Margaret Emery, May Bennett and Jean Kirk.

Miss Margaret Wilson with her bouquet and gifts on her retirement as headmistress of Westbourne House School, 1926. She was married in Carlisle to Dr W. Riddle of Poulton, who had served on the Poulton Urban District Council in the 1920s. They always took a great interest in the town. The next headmistress at Westbourne House was Miss A. Taylor, Miss Dudor being in charge of the kindergarten class.

The marble angel and cross commemorates Jean Stansfield, who died at the age of ten. She was a pupil at Westbourne House, and the whole school walked to Moorland Road Cemetery to see her grave. Jean's parents came from Rossendale and lived on Blackpool Old Road opposite Mr and Mrs W. Hodgson of The Sycamores. They purchased land, once part of the 12 acres of glebe land held by Richard Fleetwood in 1617, and presented it to the council. A recreational area was made for children, but until the 1960s swings were tied together on Sundays so that they could not be used.

The Breck, *c.* 1930. Motor car DE 4697 heads towards home from the railway station at the top of Breck Road, built after the fatal crash in 1892. This new passenger station cost £6,000 in 1896.

Rose Cottage, Breck Road in the 1950s, the home of music hall artiste Tessie O'Shea. As a celebrity she was invited to many local events, and was present with Terry Thomas at the opening of Moorland Sports Club in 1950.

Sports day at Hodgson Secondary School in the 1950s, when prizes and trophies were presented by Percy Lord, Director of Education for Lancashire. Headmaster Mr Farrand (right) is on the other side of Mrs Huddleston, the lady holding the bouquet.

Hodgson School opened on 12 November 1932 under Headmaster Mr Farrand, with staff who included Mr Gaskins (English), J. Swarbrick (Woodwork), E. Melrose (Science), O. Riding (Domestic Science), D. Evans (Geography) and Mr Ramsbottom (Art). After the Second World War it was decided to hold an annual commemoration service in November. The first speech day was held in 1950, the year in which the school magazine appeared.

Mrs Strickland of Poulton on her 90th birthday, 1950. Her daughter remembered the heat from 90 candles on the birthday cake, and that by the time the last ones were lit the first ones had melted. In 1845 three members of the Croft family lived until 92, 94 and 90 years of age, William being the eldest.

Roberta Mary Long's wedding 80 years ago, with her bridesmaid Nellie Snape standing on the left. The garden wall was the back wall of Poulton tithe-barn, a sheltered spot ideal for growing Jerusalem artichokes, which were used for pies in the baker's shop to which this garden was attached.

Mr Wrightson, who later became headmaster of Carleton School, shepherds children across Hardhorn Road on their way to school dinner, 1951. The Little Shop (right), adjoining property which was built in the 18th century, was run by Mr Foster, grocer. On the corner is the site of the old court house. H.S. Reed's grocer's shop had replaced Parkinson's, and next door to that was Lyons' jeweller's shop.

Hardhorn Road, once called Sheaf or Wheatsheaf Street because of the Wheatsheaf Inn, is in a better state than it was in the 1850s. It was then reported as disgraceful, especially in front of the school area, with 'mud more than a foot deep. A cartload of ashes was put down to form a causeway where people could cross and the first flagged area was called New Pavement.'

Mr H. Porter, a master at Baines School, kept a diary of Poulton events in those days. He was also registrar of births and deaths, newspaper correspondent, Sunday school superintendent and overseer. He died in March 1871.

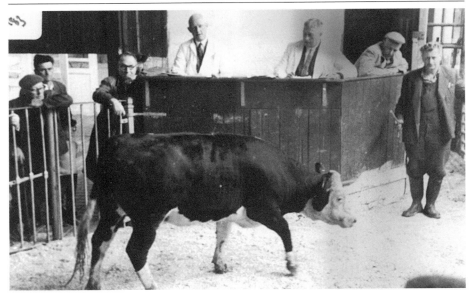

The Auction Mart behind the Golden Ball, 1960s. The first white-coated man on the left is Mr Bennet, Poulton butcher. The best-known auctioneer in the 1930s was R. Tracey Heywood, who balanced on the pens as he auctioned. Tommy Atkinson drove the cattle to auction from the station slade (ramp) behind Victoria Road.

The tithe-barn, 1960. Before the commutation of tithes in the 1830s, farmers had to bring a tenth of their harvest and animals to the agents of the lord of the manor at the tithe-barn. Tithes were not easy to collect, especially in the form of bees and their honey, and it was more convenient to pay the amount in money.

Poulton Club Day, 1923. A decorated float with girls from Sheaf Street National School makes for Queen's Square and Lower Green to join the main procession.

Poulton Gala, 1935. Five contestants for prizes in the procession are gathered at the junction of Princess Avenue, Lower Green; among them is Jenny Hesketh, who attended a private school in Poulton.

Chapel Street, 1960s. This is one of the original seven streets in a town that dates back to Saxon times. On the left is Parkinson Tomlinson's corn mill. When this was demolished, mill stones lay on the site until retrieved by Mr Walter Heapey, who put them on show at Marsh Mill, Thornton.

The Manor, built on the old moorland (Moorland Road) was at one time occupied by Fylde property developer Benjamin Corless Sykes. He moved there from Eryngo Lodge, which in 1902 became Cleveleys Hydro, and kept an eye on progress at Cleveleys through a telescope at the top of The Manor.

The demolition of Carr's Cottage, Tithebarn Street, 1970s. Old premises in Poulton were condemned in the early 1960s. Remaining cottages like this, where victims of the typhus fever outbreak of 1826–7 and the cholera epidemic of 1831–2 once lived were pulled apart and burned, the bricks alone being salvaged. Before Blackpool and Fleetwood came into being, the principal drapers and shoemakers of the Fylde had premises at Poulton where they enjoyed good trade. Thus, every cottage and penthouse continued to be occupied with structure unchanged until Poulton became more of a residential town and in 1900 was declared an Urban District. The newly added districts of Carleton and Hardhorn led to increased council membership of up to fifteen. The sewerage scheme costing £74,000 was also made necessary by November 1934.

Further demolition in Tithebarn Street, 1970s. 'For Sale – Timber Doors' reads the notice. These and other fittings were sold before the houses were dismantled by Mr Roskell's firm 'The Drop It'. Eventually the council speeded up the process, but delay had drawn attention to fine features doomed to extinction. Note the stone surround of this front door, the graceful fanlight and elegant twelve-paned windows with their slender glazing bars. In this three-storey Georgian house lived Dr Bowness, son of the Revd Robert Bowness who was a curate in Poulton for 24 years. He died in 1843.

'Peggy's shop' on Higher Green, a small general store that sold everything from sweets to fire lighters, comes down, 1970s. It was situated opposite Ike Ishmay's scrapyard, the boundary walls of which bulged dangerously with the weight of old scrap iron.

The making of Queensway between Blackpool Old Road and Tithebarn Street, early 1970s. A sheep trotting across the new road from what remained of Butler's Farm behind newly built property on Rutland Avenue indicates that even as late as this the town retained some rural aspects. On the left is the new library.

Poulton-le-Fylde Urban District Council, 1934–5. Back row, left to right: J.K. Thomas (Medical Officer), H.B. Byram, A.B. Bithell, J. Taylor, S. Woolnough. Middle row: T.M. Sharples, R.M. Smith, F. Wood, A. Kidd-Whittaker, J. Carrabine, S. Hanham. Front row: R.D. Paley (Clerk), R. Eaves, J.P. Dobson, W. Haslam (Chairman; see p. 39), R. Parkinson-Tomlinson, J. Coupe, W.G. Woolley (Surveyor). An interesting point about this civic photograph is that the Medical Officer of Health could not be present, so his photograph was superimposed later.

Poulton Urban District Council, the first chairman of which was William Hodgson (later to be knighted), came into being in 1900 and continued until 1974, when under local government re-organisation it became part of the Wyre Borough Council. Councillor J.P. Dobson, a joiner and undertaker who lived on Tithebarn Street, served for 43 years. He had arrived from Hambleton in 1887.

William Yates RN, 1941. Born on 28 November 1917 in a room over Long's baker's shop, he attended Sheaf Street School, Baines Grammar School and Goldsmith's College. He joined the Navy in 1940, his first ship being HMS *Hood*. Bill was one of 13 men suddenly transferred to shore to undergo a promotion course, and 13 proved a lucky number when HMS *Hood* sailed on her last, fateful voyage. She was sunk by the Germans in May 1941 with great loss of life. Bill was given command of ARB *Muskeeta*, a converted American motor yacht for air and sea rescue, and was involved in the Arromanches invasion. After many years teaching he retired in 1979, and, as one of Poulton's senior citizens, visited China in 1995.

The headmaster of Poulton Church of England School (formerly Sheaf Street School) shakes hands with Bishop Hoskyns Abrahall of Lancaster. The Revd T.J. Stretch, vicar of St Chad's, looks on. The occasion was the completion of phase one of a building plan in 1957, when three infant classrooms were opened. Phase two involved additional corridors to enlarge the premises and make the movement of classes safer. The school opened in 1830 and has played a great part in the life of the town. Early galas were organised almost entirely through this school, every scholar taking part. Gardening classes were then a feature, as at Carleton and Singleton, because many boys took agricultural jobs and the girls often worked as dairy maids.

This view of Poulton-le-Fyle in the 1960s shows that great changes had taken place in the structure of the town. The tithe-barn had been demolished, the last of the derelict thatched cottages and three-storey Georgian houses in Tithebarn Street had been pulled down, and the large area of Butler's Farm had been cleared to make way for the Teanlowe shopping centre. The weekly auction at the cattle market held in the pens behind the Golden Ball still continued, but its days were numbered. Over the house-tops of Tithebarn Street can be seen the 60.97 acres at Carleton Green released by the Department of the Environment for residential development. Although building by Norwest Housing did not commence until 1973, a folder containing redevelopment plans was soon on sale at Entwistle and Company, estate agents. The volume of traffic through the town had increased dramatically, and the old approach shown in the photograph was to be replaced by a one-way system and eventually a traffic-free area in Market Square.

Poulton was an example of the modern growth of the Fylde. At the 1931 Census, the population was 3,366. In 1934 the boundaries of the Urban District had been extended and pre-war population was estimated at 6,000, but by 1972 had reached 16,280.

Folk dancing in Market Square, 1978. This group, which includes Mr William Yates and the late Mrs Yates, invited the public to join in the Circassian Circle. They also ran a weekly class. Dancing round the Maypole was traditional at Lower Green, and morris dancing was a feature of all Fylde galas. For centuries farmers had been renowned for their agility and staying powers at barn dances when Harvest Home was celebrated. The Farmers' Ball was held at the Winter Gardens, Blackpool in later years. Young men who had to walk all the way home to Garstang or Poulton arrived at 5 a.m. 'in time for the milking'.

St Chad's Church in the background, although not mentioned in Domesday Book, may date from 1094, but some historians believe that an insignificant wooden church would be in existence long before William the Conqueror's men were sent to make a survey of all England. The graveyard was crammed with tombstones going back to the early 18th century until it was closed for burials and more recently 'tidied'. Before the graves were swept away, a careful record of their whereabouts was made, and this is available in Poulton Library. The churchyard is famed for its spring display of crocuses, and the tall trees once had a considerable rookery. Four fine sycamores fronted the churchyard, but when these were wantonly cut down in the early 19th century a wide ditch was revealed. May this have originated centuries ago as a moat like that at Hambleton Church, which was built on the site of the old manor house?

The Joseph Cross Memorial Convalescent Home, 1933. Members of the cotton industry from all over Lancashire could recuperate here after illness. This became Poulton-le-Fylde College of Education and latterly the Civic Centre for the Borough of Wyre.

The Mary Macarthur Home on Breck Road was also a convalescent home until the 1980s, when it became a home for the elderly. This view dates from the 1940s.

Athletic Sports at Hogdson Secondary School, 6 June 1951. Mrs J.B. Hull presented the trophies. Headmaster Mr Farrand (left) watches as the Silcock Shield for the Winning House is handed over. The Houses were Angles (red), Danes (blue) and Saxons (yellow). For a number of years in the 1950s Saxons dominated.

Freedom From Hunger Year, 1963. Poulton raised over £1,000 at many events, mainly hunger lunches. Left to right: C. Rothwell (Secretary), Mr G. Hill (teacher), Jane Inman (Sheaf Street scholar), Mr W. Clarkson (Headmaster), Mrs Muir (Oxfam), Mr Finch, Mrs Melville, -?-. This presentation was made in the Church Hall, Vicarage Road.

A line-up of young cellists, some from the Fylde Academy for Young Musicians in Poulton, 1967. They were competing at the Lytham Music Festival. First on the left is Martin Milner, who won first prize; fifth left is Philip Quinlan. Many went on to join the Lancashire Youth Orchestra.

Two pupils leave the College of Education on 18 March 1972, where the Fylde Academy for Young Musicians was directed by Dennis Brookes with tutors Grace Leslie, Harry George, Glyn Lloyd and 'Dougie' Drake. Trombonist Martin Kelly (rear) later played for the London show *Starlight Express*.

Bill Gorst, School Manager, retired Poulton Church of England School teacher Mrs Dorothy Ainsworth and Headmaster Bill Clarkson, surrounded by some of the school's pupils, 1970s. Among them are Helen Reid, Andrew Green, Alison Rooney, Jennifer Unsworth and Jennifer Golby. Mrs Ainsworth had come back to give out prizes on Sports Day. Built in 1830 as a national school and used also as a Sunday school, over the years it has undergone many changes – and the name Sheaf Street has become Hardhorn Road.

Old record books kept by headmasters reveal varied activity. On 24 March 1911 Standard III, having 100 per cent attendance, went for a nature walk. In May 1911 blossom was outstanding so the whole school paraded the lanes. In November of that year school was closed for six weeks because of a measles outbreak. The First World War years featured blackberrying; in 1918 2 cwt 9 lbs were collected, the proceeds going to war relief, aided by sales of work. Headmaster John Winchester, a keen cricketer, arrived in 1921; in 1928 110 infants were still being taught in one room. Mr P. Vause, a teacher, was given leave to play for Blackburn Rovers in a 1937 Cup Replay; and 200 evacuees arrived in 1939.

The Mayor of Wyre, Poulton Councillor Charles F. Stebbing who had been Chairman of the Urban District Council in 1964, accompanied Sir Walter Clegg, MP for the District of Wyre, to a fish auction at Fleetwood Docks. Sir Walter stands between the two men in white coats. There was much concern about the demise of the fish industry. Under 1974 local government re-organisation Fleetwood, Thornton, Garstang and Poulton amalgamated to become the Borough of Wyre, whose boundaries stretched as far as the Bleasdale Fells.

In earlier days, as Blackpool grew it wished to annex Poulton, but there was fierce opposition to this plan. Over centuries local administration in Poulton has passed from the sworn men of Elizabeth I's day, when the parochial vestry appointed its parish constables, overseers and surveyors, to the establishment of the parish council and the formation of an urban district in 1900. The urban district area was extended on 1 April 1934 when 707 acres from Carleton and 776 acres from Hardhorn-with-Newton were added.

Hodgson High School had a picture of guide dog 'Quiz' presented in gratitude from the Guide Dogs for the Blind Association in 1978, yet another to add to their collection. On this occasion a representative of the association (left) visited the school with his guide dog.

Market Square became a traffic-free zone in 1984, and the war memorial was moved from Queen's Square. Catherine Rothwell, local historian and retired Poulton librarian, checks on her Town Trail designed for the increasing numbers of visitors. On the right are the refurbished premises of the county police.

# CARLETON, THORNTON, BISPHAM, LAYTON

*Thornton village, 1901.*

The old Carleton School, *c.* 1890. Its shuttered windows and boundary wall made of cobbles from the seashore can be seen. The school was built in 1839. The founder, Elizabeth Wilson of Whiteholme, near Carleton, left money in her will of 1680 for the education of the poor.

Hawthorne Road, Thornton, 1882. Thatched cruck cottage, seashore cobbles, unpaved lane and heavy farm cart are signs from rural life a century ago, but brick-built houses with slate roofs were appearing.

Carleton Gala, 1912. This little group in ribbons and lace pulled by Daisy the mare (even her blinkers are decorated with rosebuds) has won first prize in its section. Great and Little Carleton looked forward all year to the occasion. The rose queen and retinue had their own landau, polished to perfection, lamps gleaming. Mothers sat up all night making paper roses to cover floats and the big, wrought-iron archway at Castle Gardens Hotel. Morris dancers performed along the processional route. Their trainer, Billy Livesey, a tailor, dressed them in white tunics with green sashes. As a boy, Billy had been a member of the Carleton troupe.

The procession assembled outside Carleton School at Four Lane Ends and moved off, led by Poulton Brass Band, finishing at Mustow's Field or Pye's Farm, Carleton Lodge where the maypole was kept. Norcross Farm rewarded more dancing with cakes, biscuits and ginger beer.

The courtyard of Castle Gardens Inn, ideally sited at the ancient Four Lane Ends, *c.* 1894. Here farmers and agricultural workers gathered to compare notes. The hotel was owned by Catterall and Swarbrick, who supplied nearly all the inns and hotels in the area. From left to right, the group of men are -?-, Jim Beavers, John Brown, Fred Sprowell, -?-, Jimmy Hull, Bobby Hull, Tom Brough, Tom Cookson – all local men. The horse answered to the name of Dobbin. John Brown had a farm on Fleetwood Road opposite Savile Avenue, now entirely built up. In his youth Fred Sprowell emigrated to Russia, and when he returned lived at 41 Blackpool Road. The brothers Jimmy and Bobby Hull lived next door but one to Fred Sprowell and Tom Cookson rented Rinkton Cottage. The neighbourliness within a small community is epitomised in this study from last century. Carleton Marsh, situated on the coast between Bispham and Thornton, was reclaimed in about 1800. This was a long-established family community with 30 farms, some very old. Prospect Farm had a stone plaque dated 1670. John Walsh of Marsh Farm was the first in the Fylde to experiment with guano, and his improved results interested Bold Fleetwood Hesketh, lord of the manor. A public trial of mowing machines was held in 1868, and Mr Eden demonstrated on James Fairclough's land with its luxuriant crop of clover.

Carleton Bowling Club, 1916. Third from the left in the middle row is Thomas Carter, resident signalman at Carleton Crossing. Mrs Carter had crowned the Gala queen on one occasion, and grandfather William became a police sergeant. As children, all attended Carleton School.

The bowling green of Carleton Ladies' Bowling Club, formerly Leach Meadow, 1915. A number of wounded soldiers had been invited to Carleton. They were probably being nursed at the Vicarage, Poulton, as this was made into a small military hospital during the First World War.

Morris dancers ready for Carleton Gala, 1927. Standing first and second left are the Cookson brothers, with Wilf Davis third. At the back is their trainer, Billy Livesey.

This float, with Kitty Gleave as the Fairy Queen, won third prize at the Carleton Gala in 1929. Kitty became Mrs Greenhalgh. The Gala queen travelled by landau and was crowned under the wrought-iron arch at Castle Gardens.

At this point Kitty Gleave and retinue are passing Carleton Garage, whose owner Oliver Stokes is in the taxi, 1929. John Carrabine, who had the newsagent's shop before the Brooks, was also a hairdresser and was always busy at Gala time.

Castle Gardens Hotel, 1890s. The Weld Arms had become the Castle Hotel in about 1890, but when Arthur Fitzroy Thompson arrived as victualler he introduced pleasure grounds and accommodation for visitors. Captain Thompson created tea rooms, a small zoo, swing boats, well-laid-out gardens and bowling green. Strawberry and cream teas drew the wagonette parties.

W.H. Brook, Carleton newsagent and stationer in the 1920s. This is now Gleave's newsagent's. Besides selling paints, pots, papers, and so on, it held a Lancashire County Library centre one day a week. The original tin-plate sign bearing the torch was found in an upper room some years ago. Next door was Henderson's Dining Room and fish and chip shop. Bowler's General Store was where children bought 'penn'orths' and 'ha'porths' of bull's-eyes, liquorice bats, jelly babies, kali, and 'ducks and greenpeas'. Across the road was the turnstile entry for the Castle Gardens (admission 2*d*). A temperance hut on the forecourt outside the gardens catered for tea drinkers from the wagonette parties – those who had 'signed the pledge' and promised never to let 'raging strong drink' pass their lips. Yet another entrance to the wonderful world of the gardens was through the ironmonger's shop opposite Brook's.

The Tithe Commutation Award for Great and Little Carleton was drawn up in 1838 when Great Moss Field was an isolated pasture. The complete skeleton of a male elk was discovered here in 1970. Referred to as the High Furlong elk, the animal must have been attacked and pursued, escaping to die in a pond. Pollen analysis shows that this happened in winter, when the pond iced over and the body was entombed. Covered by lake sediments, after thousands of years it was revealed when building took place.

Thornton post office, 1905. John Ashton (see also pp. 82 and 87) ran the post office at Thornton in 1880, for which he was paid £5 a year. He built this double-fronted house and business premises for the family. One son had a clog shop at the back and part was let as a bank. Charles Ashton stands by the railings.

Thornton, 1905. Marsh Mill was built by Bold Fleetwood Hesketh in 1794. In the background are the drying kiln for the corn, listed in the Tithe Commutation and Schedules of 1838, and the mill cottages, all of which were later pulled down.

Robert Hawthornthwaite, miller of Marsh Mill, *c.* 1909. For generations various grades of flour had been ground, but at the turn of the century the demand was for finely milled white flour which was beyond the mill's capability. Until 1930 meal was ground only for farm use; eventually this also ceased and the mill was used as a café. A tragic accident involving the death of two ladies led to the mill's closure for a number of years, until it was bought by Thornton Urban District Council and preservation work was carried out by Walter Heapey and enthusiastic supporters. Exhibitions were held and restoration work continued. On 23 August 1979 the Mayor of Wyre, Alderman Grime, with the Duke of Westminster present, opened an ambitious shopping complex built around the Marsh Mill.

In Robert Hawthornthwaite's day fine horses were brought to the mill smithy, alongside which was Jack Breakell's wheelwright's shop. Not far away Atkinson's meadow, reaching down to the river, was filled with stooks of corn at harvest time.

John Ashton, when he was aged 81, March 1946. Behind him Thornton Mill is dwarfing the row of cottages known as Mill Terrace. Born in 1865, it was Mr Ashton who built the Thornton post office premises in 1905 and carried on in the job until 1939; his son Charles took over until 1957. Thornton was originally a large township extending from half a mile outside Poulton-le-Fylde to the port of Fleetwood, and the postal work was extensive – with four deliveries and collections a day. Before post offices were built, hotels and posting houses were used, the nearest to Thornton in 1882 being the Cleveleys Hotel run by Martha Gardner.

The Old Mill, Thornton, 1927, was a favourite picture postcard to send home. At the time of Queen Victoria's Golden Jubilee, Marsh Mill, erected by millwright Ralph Slater, was whitewashed and the sails and fan painted. A custom observed by more than one miller in 'Windmill Land' was to stop the sails in the form of a cross when a funeral was passing.

The old practice of 'wake' at a windmill developed from the fear of fire. When winds were strong the whirling sails could overheat the machinery and send out potentially destructive sparks. In the Fylde, hand-made cogs of apple-tree wood were favoured for smooth running.

The miller had to be skilled in dressing the millstones and controlling the speed of the sails. The cap of Marsh Mill, tarred and shaped like an upturned boat, was designed to turn bodily in order to keep the sails into the wind. In 1895 the cast-iron wind shaft replaced one made of timber. Mr Johnson was the first miller at Thornton and Mr Hawthornthwaite the last. This was the end of a long line, bearing in mind that there was first mention of a mill at Thornton in 1295.

Thornton Gala passes Marsh Mill and the post office on Mill Terrace, 1912. On the left was Woodlands Avenue; on the right, Pleasant Grove, sometimes called 'Gypsy Row'. Croasdale Terrace and Willow Grove, where a Maltese had a cycle shop, were nearby.

Herbert Ashton, the youth in the straw hat, is amongst the decorated bicycle contingent at Thornton Festival, 1912. George Graham is on his left, a character who enjoyed dressing up for any occasion. In 1935 Herbert went to work in Peru.

Thornton Gala, 1915. The procession approaches from the railway station crossing. Fashions in clothes, bicycles, prams and lamps all feature in this busy scene. Especially interesting is the pre-First World War motor car.

Victoria Road, Thornton, 1915. On the left is 'Teapot Row', so called because the residents always had the kettle on the boil ready for brew-up. On the right in Victoria Road East is the Wignall Memorial Methodist Church.

Thornton for Cleveleys station, 1915. A train approaches the level crossing. Formerly called Ramper Road, which was the old 18th-century name for Victoria Road, this was the stop for boys going to Rossall School. Some of them, like Patrick Campbell, came from Ireland.

Rossall Road, Cleveleys, 1906. Howarth's butcher's shop is on the left, and the two butchers stand outside by the cobbled walls that stretch the length of this terrace.

John Ashton, 1885. As a young man he took his penny-farthing bicycle on one of the Isle of Man Steam Packet boats sailing from Fleetwood. John cycled all his life (see p. 82), as did his son and grandson, covering the Fylde lanes and beyond to Bleasdale Fells. He lived until he was 93. In 1891 he married a lady from Grantham who, as a nanny, had brought two boys up to Rossall School for their education. She remained to keep an eye on them at the request of the boys' parents in Grantham and she met John at Thornton post office.

John and Annie Louisa Ashton, c. 1895. John was born in 1865 and died in 1957. Annie was born in 1868 and died in 1950. The children, from left to right, are J. Scott (born 1894), Charles (born April 1892 and died April 1989), Grace (born 1893 and died 1976). Scott Ashton wrote an interesting history of St Chad's Church, published in 1949. John, the father, attended school half time, working on a farm in the afternoon. At 19 he had his own shoe-making shop in Thornton village, but after 20 years took charge of the post office. The Ashtons were a family of nine, who kept a cow and reared a pig each year for killing in the autumn.

Burn Naze Crossing, seen here in 1900, was unmanned until 1926 when a tragedy occurred, in which a manager from Imperial Chemical Industries Works was killed. Thereafter, Dick Woods and Edward Gleeson were employed to be in attendance at the crossing.

A motor train at Burn Naze Halt early this century. The station, with its small booking office, solitary lamp and Lancashire and Yorkshire Railway iron sign, was near the United Alkali Works. A house in the grounds, occupied by the Gregson family, was demolished in about 1920 when a bridge was built at Burn Naze Crossing.

Burn Naze football team, 1929. Back row, left to right: J. Murtagh, J. Riley, J. Bamber, A. Power, J. Gara, F. Hargreaves, T. Curley, T. Gleeson. Front row: M. Power, D. Flanagan, D. Osman, J. Irvine (Fleetwood's mace bearer), H. Ward.

United Alkali Works cricket team, Thornton, 1919. Centre, with pads and cricket bat, is Dan Connolly. Beside him with dog on his knee is J. Lavery. The two seated cricketers at the front are J. Edwards and J. Feeney. The fourth man from the left on the back row is J. Dooney.

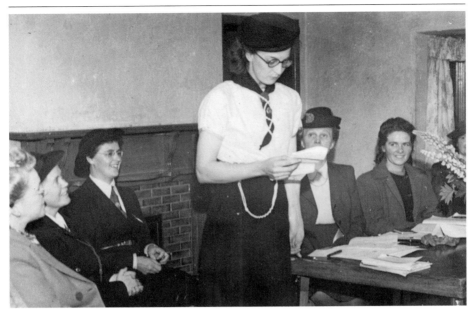

In May 1945 the First Thornton Girl Guides Annual General Meeting was attended by, left to right, Mrs Keirby, Mrs Darcy Leigh (District Commissioner), Margaret Horne (Sea Ranger), Mrs R.O. Nickson, Miss Patricia Watson (District Secretary) and Mrs Taylor (District Treasurer).

In the summer of 1940, shortly after the outbreak of the Second World War, Local Defence Volunteers gathered at Thornton Lecture Hall with whatever weapons they could muster. Second on the left, back row, is Charles Ashton, who later joined the Royal Engineers.

The inauguration of Lancashire Library Mobile Library Service, based at Thornton-le-Fylde, 1950. Left to right: County Councillor Lumb, Mrs Pennistan, Lady Openshaw, Miss E. Ashworth (Branch Librarian), Mr Grundy (Chairman of the Council), Mrs Grundy, County Councillor J.R. Hull, Miss F.E. Cook (County Librarian), Mr A.H. Catterall (former headmaster of Beach Road School).

Miss Patricia Watson (left), Assistant Librarian in 1950, meets a Fylde lady at Wrea Green whose favourite author, she declared, was 'Baroness O'Crazy', and if there were none of the Baroness's books then she would not accept anything else. She meant Baroness Orczy, who wrote the famous series about the Scarlet Pimpernel. Roses round the door and the wearing of clogs remained hallmarks of the Fylde area. The Mobile Library Service, for over 40 years a boon to far-flung cottages and farms, had its services curtailed by today's recession.

Bispham smithy, with wheelwright's shop attached where carts were mended and ploughshares and coulters sharpened, late 19th century. Bispham was a small village of whitewashed dwellings, all of which have now been demolished. The 17th-century thatched cottages, farms, saddler's shop, village shop (famous for treacle), the Ivy Cottage Tea Rooms, ancient church, and an inn, supplemented by visits from the pedlar and the travelling tailor in his pony and trap, meant that Bispham was self-supporting.

In All Hallows Road between church and village centre was the bow-windowed Red Lion Inn, run by Frederick Fitzroy Thompson and known locally as the 'Red Cat'. On the snowy morning of 22 December 1894 the New Brunswick timber ship *Abana* was wrecked off Little Bispham. The crew of 17, including Captain Danielson and the ship's dog, were rescued by the lifeboat *Samuel Fletcher* and taken to the Red Lion.

Bispham Church Sunday school bible class motor trip with the church and school house in the background, 6 May 1914. Two crowded motor charabancs are ready for off, possibly to The Grapes at Wrea Green. Longer trips were made by train.

Bispham Church, 1962. In this church, All Hallows, the Revd William Thornber was married in 1831 by the Revd Charles Hesketh, brother of the lord of the manor. Charles lived at Bispham Lodge until he was appointed to the living at St Chad's in Poulton. He did not stay long, however, preferring Churchtown near Southport, where he later resided at Meols Hall.

Norbreck when the tram track was under construction, early 20th century. Norbreck Hall Hydro, as it was then called, is in the background. Was the tramroad a light railway? Argument went as far as the House of Lords, which in 1907 said it was – which settled the 'Tramroad Rating' question.

Norbreck Road leading to the shore, 1913, little changed compared with a century earlier, as can be seen from the thatched longhouse (right) with its whitewashed, cobble-stone garden walls.

Norbreck Hydro Swimming Baths or Lido was officially opened in the winter of 1931 by Councillor G.N. Hardcastle of Manchester, when T.H. Shorrocks was Manager. The pool, 60 ft by 27 ft with pink-cream walls, had a mosaic floor coloured turquoise and amethyst.

Miss Alys (Alice) Milner (far right), Beauty Queen of the North employed by the Poulton firm Windsor Woollies (see also p. 98), led a parade of girls in beach pyjamas when the Norbreck Swimming Bath was opened in 1931.

Layton Road, early 1930s. To make way for road widening some of these buildings were scheduled for demolition. The whitewashed cottage on the corner was over 200 years old and the shop on the left, a long-established provision dealer, had been there when the road was one of the main thoroughfares into Blackpool. John Gratrix was the last miller at nearby Hoo Hill or Wheelmill, when in July 1881 a severe storm ruined crops, put roads under water and lightning struck the mill and farm. Two sails were hurled into the fields. The tower mill, originally a peg mill, had been erected in 1736 using bricks from a local croft.

Another member of the Gratrix family, George of Hardhorn, bought the Hall at Whinney Heys where his son John farmed. The Revd William Thornber, in his *History of Blackpool and Neighbourhood*, relates how this son, on his way back from market, was murdered in Old Meadow Lane, Hardhorn. As the culprit was never found, villagers believed the area to be haunted. The ancient highway to Poulton passed Hoo Hill Mill.

Layton Road, October 1935. The fingerpost points to Poulton. The thatched roof of the longhouse was covered with corrugated iron to keep out the rain. Everything, including sweets, sugar, treacle, oatmeal and paraffin, was sold at the village general store.

The kitchen at Layton Hall was demolished on 13 September 1927. Little of this historic Fylde house was saved apart from the gateposts surmounted with carved stone pineapples, which now grace Stanley Park. Layton Hall was the main residence of Alexander Rigby in the 18th century, but as roads were impassable in winter he used his town house situated opposite the stocks in Poulton. The old manor house was sold by William Fleetwood to Edward Rigby in the late 16th century, and with it the tithes of grain in Layton, Warbreck and the 'Pool'. One enterprising member of the family traded abroad, where he died in prison after falling heavily into debt.

A bevy of Windsor Woolly Mannequins led by chief mannequin Alys Milner, 1930s. This family firm called on their staff to model swimsuits and other garments. By the 1930s the Windsor area representatives were covering the whole country, and a nationwide reputation for first-class knitwear had been established (see p. 11). A new two-storey factory in Buchanan Street, Blackpool was leased. With pioneer Benjamin on the watch for high quality, should any garment fail to reach his high standards, he 'put his scissors through it'. A factory designed specifically for the manufacture of Windsor (Regd) Woollies, with room for expanding output, was built at Castle Works, Poulton-le-Fylde.

In 1931 the young princesses Elizabeth and Margaret Rose were presented with Windsor Woolly garments at the British Industries Fair, and the following year saw a new line, quality and elegance in swimwear. The opening ceremonies at new swimming pools in coastal resorts and cities up and down the country were graced by this bevy of bathing beauties.

Windsor Water Woollies featured in films and stage shows. Castle Works was extended to double production and within the space of seven years output had quadrupled. Here the girls are parading at St Anne's-on-the-Sea, the colour scheme of their swimwear being maroon and white.

Tram 79 is specially numbered 118 to distinguish it from the regular service, although it followed the same route, to carry a crowd of holidaymakers along the Fylde coast from Fleetwood to Starr Gate, early 1920s. Men considered Lancashire flat cloth caps *de rigueur* for work or play. Fortunately the girls had more imagination in their headgear.

Trams in Bispham, 1907. To make way for Bispham tram track, Pat's Pantry, previously known as The Cliff, had to be demolished in the 1930s. Quack doctor T. Worden sold remedies on the beach to visitors when he lived at The Cliffs.

Blackpool Golf Club Secretary Neil Green (left) and golf professional James Albert Steer, with the club house in the background, 1924. Mr Steer was renowned for his club-manufacturing business, which employed a staff of three working on jiggers and mashie niblicks. Wooden clubs then cost £1 each and irons 16s 6d. Bags of clubs were stored in his shop, and for an annual fee clubs were kept clean by constant use of emery and grease, before the days of stainless steel.

He competed in the northern section of the Professional Golfers' Association at Leeds in 1922, assisted at Lytham St Anne's before it was designated 'Royal', designed seven new holes for Blackpool, and also used his design skills at Fairhaven and Fleetwood golf courses.

The great golfer Harry Vardon, six times winner of the Open Championship, drives off at Blackpool Golf Club, 1908. By the 1920s knee breeches had been ousted in popularity by plus-fours. This photograph has been reprinted from an original glass plate negative.

A competition in progress on the Sandhill Links, situated on the west side of the railway near the tramway to St Anne's-on-the-Sea, c. 1925. By 1930 a holiday camp covered most holes, and in 1939 the links had to give way for the construction of Blackpool Airport.

Whitegate Drive Baptist Church, 1920. In 1875 the Union Baptist Church was situated on the present site of the post office in Abingdon Street. All the Baptist churches jointly commemorated the 85th birthday of local Baptist minister the Revd Samuel Pilling, who attended the famous C.H. Spurgeon's Baptist College.

Blackpool Congregational Choir, 1950. They were celebrating the Alexandra Road Church Jubilee of 1900–50. Commencing with the first building, Bethesda Chapel, in 1825, moving to Victoria Street in 1850 and to Alexandra Road in the 1920s, the Congregational Church Choir had won the trophies at Lytham Festival.

When Blackpool sands were clean and golden they were enjoyed by locals as well as visitors. This photograph dates from August 1906. The donkeys wintered on farms in Poulton-le-Fylde and Hambleton. One day each year children from Carleton School were walked along the winding lane past Whiteholme to the beach. Cecil Milner is the small boy holding the hat.

SS *Cleveleys* was one of a number of pleasure steamers that sailed along the Fylde coast during the summer season in the early years of the twentieth century.

The laying of the foundation stone at the Congregational Church in Agnew Road, Fleetwood, 1937. From left to right: R. Garnett, Charles Riley, William Brown (builder), Dr Preston.

Brown and Jackson of Elm Street, Fleetwood, established 1908, display old and new style stair rails, 1933. This was one of the tableaux at Fleetwood Carnival and Poulton Gala. The Browns' house, which was flooded in 1927 when the sea engulfed the town, became the works offices.

# ST MICHAEL'S, OVER-WYRE, SKIPPOOL, SINGLETON

*St Michael's-on-Wyre Church, 1925. An ancient foundation dating from the year 640, it was rebuilt in Henry VIII's reign. The clock in the tower was presented to the vicar, the Revd Hugh P. Hornby, in the 1920s. This photograph is taken from part of a local schoolboy's 1925 collage.*

The Mason family after a game of croquet, summer 1880. At the back is James, with Mr Mason senior beside him. Centre, left to right: Grace Roe, Mrs Nellie Mason, Hannah Roe Mason (wife of James Mason senior). They were a farming family from Stalmine. In the 1870s the draining of Rawcliffe and Pilling mosses was still in progress, and for this important process, which transformed bog into fine arable land, tile and brick works up and down the Fylde were financed by the chief landowners.

WITH GOOD LUCK.

John Nicholson, cousin to Peter Nicholson, served in the Lancers in the Boer War. This Victorian 'good luck' card entwined with ivy leaves was sent home to Staynall following the relief of Ladysmith on 28 February 1900, the last major war in which these light cavalrymen played a part. The quadrille known as The Lancers, which was popular at Victorian balls, came into fashion in 1850.

St. Michael's-on-Wyre, 1920s. First on the left is a small farm with barn attached, then the Grapes Inn where Christopher Rowson was landlord. This is just before the old bridge spanning the River Wyre, over which Bonnie Prince Charlie's army marched in 1745.

Floods at St Michael's-on-Wyre, when the river overflowed its banks, 1980. The cottages at the far end of this row were so undermined that two had to be taken down.

A wagonette party setting off, 11 August 1908. Parties like this one went all over the Fylde taking visitors to see the windmills, the stocks and tithe-barn at Poulton, Singleton model village, the district of Over Wyre, Gull Moss, the Saracen's Head, Simpson's and innumerable strawberry gardens and inns where stops were made for refreshment. This group, with a Carleton man in attendance, is outside Oliver's Boot and Shoe Warehouse, Blackpool, 'the largest retailer of boots in the world'.

Once this group left Blackpool, the first extensive view of the Fylde was from Hoo Hill, then on to Poulton. Here, outside the Black Bull with its own brew house, trippers might be encouraged to sit with their legs in the stocks for an itinerant photographer, Maynard Tomlinson or Mr C. Lord, who would have results ready when travellers returned in the evening. Stalmine with its Grange where peaches grew on high brick walls warmed by charcoal heating, the smell of burning peat, the heavy scent of hawthorn blossom in spring and the clacking of windmills must have been pleasant enticements. This mode of transport offered wide views over the countryside but there were dangers. The wagonettes were known to overturn, as did one breasting the hill near Burn Hall early this century.

A postman collects mail from a Victorian letter box near Thistleton, *c.* 1893. Long distances demanded a mail cart but deliveries were frequent and prompt. Letters arrived at Poulton three times daily and there were four dispatches, the last collection being at 8 p.m. In 1901 the postmaster was William Walker.

White Hall, 1960. On the banks of the River Wyre at Rawcliffe, upstream from Cartford Bridge, it had been a farm since 1860. As a manor house it belonged for centuries to the Kirkbys and Westbys, two influential Fylde families. It was rebuilt in this form by George Westby.

Shooting party at Roseacre, *c.* 1900. Second from the left is 'Owd Molecatcher'. Nobody seemed to know his real name. Holding the gun, right, is Richard Eccles. Wild duck shooting was customary at Singleton Carrs, where there were so many ducks that villagers complained of surfeit in the early 19th century.

Great Eccleston village, *c.* 1900. The Revd W.T. Bulpit believed that in medieval times the Leyland Hundred met there, resulting in two village greens. With fellow-researcher Mr Taylor he discovered the village stocks, together with the cross around which the meetings were held, in a horse pond.

Wardleys Cottage, with Mrs Hornby seated by a boat, *c.* 1900. She was one of six daughters born to William Swarbrick, who ferried between Cockle Hall and Wardleys Creek for 50 years. Born in 1816, William gathered mussels and fished for the salmon that were plentiful then in the River Wyre. The emigrant ship *Six Sisters* which sailed from Wardleys was named after his daughters.

The Fleetwood ferry boat at Knott End, *c.* 1903. At Sea Dyke Cottages close to this spot ships from Wardleys and Skippool took on sweet water (the term for fresh water), as they did at Wardleys Cottage. Tradition had it that smuggled casks of spirit from the Isle of Man were unloaded here for ferrying to Wardleys.

Thomas Roe and Mary Jane Roe of Hambleton, who were married in the 1850s. He was the great-grandfather of Mr Harry Hodgkinson, who reported, 'Great-grandfather Roe was one of twelve elders who turned the River Wyre into a north country Jordan in 1835.' Twelve 'Particular Baptists' were totally immersed in the river when embracing the faith. The Revd Samuel Pilling (see p. 102) was present. This eminent divine had letters from the great John Ruskin. Mary Jane came from Poulton, where there was a branch of the Roe family in later years (ironmongers). Their son James was head choirboy at St Chad's, and later had his own band playing at the Majestic Hotel in St Anne's.

James Poole Roe as a small boy, 1895. His family farmed at Burrows Farm on the bluff above the River Wyre just north of Wardleys Ferry. Mr Hodgkinson recalled: 'My father remembered being rowed across the ferry in the 1880s. As a youth I myself saw a fire which I was told had not been out for two hundred years. It was in the house of a family called Fisher. It was of course made of peat. Even when the house had been rebuilt the fire was transferred from the old hearth to the new. The fire was more than a means of heating people and food; it had a symbolic and even sacramental quality.'

Skippool Creek with the café on the left, 21 September 1954. Here the River Skipton entered the Wyre, draining from Marton Mere. Opposite was Wardleys, Poulton's second harbour. In the 16th and 17th centuries Russian ships called and in the 18th century there was an arrangement with a Mr Rhoe to supply ships for the Emperor of Russia, but instead of building new ships he refurbished old ones and thereafter the Russian vessels ceased trading. The port of Fleetwood was not active until 1840 but even after the removal of the customs from Poulton to Fleetwood, Wardleys remained a legal quay. As many as seven vessels might arrive. Swainsons and Birleys of Kirkham had their own quays where flax from Russia and later Ireland was unloaded. American ships brought timber, tallow, cotton and oranges.

Skippool was further known in the 17th century for possibly harbouring a witch. 'Thou art a witch and a demdyke,' William Wilkinson (alias Johnson) declared to Dorothie Shaw on 12 December 1627. Perhaps on the advice of her husband Thomas, Dorothie went to the magistrate Richard Burgh of Larbreck to deny this dangerous charge. A ducking stool was kept at the bottom of the Breck for suspected witches and nagging women. This pond was culverted in the 19th century when a dye house was built.

Jenny Hesketh of Skippool, seen here in the 1930s with Zena, her prize Alsatian, which won an award at Crufts Dog Show in London. Jenny trained and exhibited her dogs at Great Eccleston Agricultural Show, which commenced about the middle of last century when the villagers were employed in cutting rushes and preparing them for the rushlight makers. Joseph Lytham was chief rush dealer and Stephen Beckett was landlord of the Rush Cutters Inn at Elswick.

The Great Wheel erected at Blackpool, which opened for the public on 22 August 1896, could be clearly seen from Hambleton. It was a magnificent piece of structural engineering which had 30 carriages suspended around its perimeter. It could take passengers to a height of 220 ft in the air, each carriage carrying 30 people. Despite the wonderful views afforded the Big Wheel was never as popular as the Tower, and was eventually dismantled, the carriages being sold off as hen houses and offices. At Wild Boar Cottage, Rawcliffe Road, the Big Wheel Café is a carriage from the original famous wheel, the only remaining carriage in public use and a true relic.

The grave of Meg Shelton, the witch who would not lie down even when dead. Born Meg Hilton, the illegitimate child of a Singleton man, in the 18th century she was also known as Meg Sheldon. She reputedly lived on haggis, a common dish in the Fylde, which consisted of boiled groats (the grain of oats without the husks) mixed with thyme or parsley. She was said to milk the cows of Singleton, using a pitcher which would turn into a goose and walk in front of her, until one wily farmer struck the goose and it became a broken pitcher in a pool of milk. On one occasion the miller of Singleton, armed with his pitchfork, had sent her packing. A sack of corn, when pierced, turned into the witch who nimbly leapt on to her broomstick and sailed out of the mill towards the full moon. She lived at Cuckoo Hall Cottage, Wesham.

After her burial in Woodplumpton churchyard, Singleton farmers dug her up and re-buried her, head down, under this large boulder. Three times she scratched her way to the surface but was firmly re-interred and the spot exorcised by a priest.

There is no evidence that she did dabble in witchcraft, but because disasters and mishaps persisted even after her death she was still suspected by the superstitious folks around Poulton and Singleton of continuing her mischief.

St Anne's Church, Singleton, *c.* 1910. The area in front through the lych gate was carefully kept in those days with clipped box hedges and a herb garden. The church was consecrated on 12 July 1860.

Singleton fire station, 1902. This was provided by Squire J.H. Miller, along with a manually operated fire engine which was coupled to whatever horse could be pressed into service; a fire was often beyond control by the time horse and fire engine arrived.

Singleton village in the snow of 29 January 1965, a rare experience in the Fylde. The Fylde Water Board man is preparing to clear a water main; perhaps the supply was frozen. In 1940 snow buried cars and even locomotives, and there were ice floes in the harbours.

Thomas Horrocks Miller of Singleton Park, who succeeded his father Thomas Miller, lord of the manor, presented the lych gate at St Anne's Church in 1879. He also bought and gave to the church a black, oak chair which is thought to have been used by John Milton when he wrote *Paradise Lost*. Thomas Horrocks Miller was greatly interested in improving land by drainage. 'In no part of Lancashire can be found a village better laid out and cleaner than Singleton,' a newspaper report stated in 1892. He owned a prize-winning stallion named Honest Tom, and paid handsomely in golden guineas for any animal that he thought would improve his bloodstock. Wagonette parties came from Blackpool to see the 'show village' of Singleton. Pheasant and partridge, plentiful in the Fylde coverts around Hardhorn and Singleton, were on the menu at the Millers Arms. There were complaints that the quality of 'the village of shingled roofs' was being marred by 'wooden refreshment booths with corrugated iron roofs'.

Hambleton village, 1940. The name means 'the village on the bend of the river', and at this time it was still composed mainly of thatched cottages and farms, the chief inn being The Malt Shovels. In this ancient settlement the parish church of the Blessed Virgin Mary was built on the site of the Shireburn family's moated manor house, and later Hambleton Primary School was built on part of the drained moat. Originally a chapel-of-ease for Kirkham, the church of the Blessed Virgin Mary became a church in its own right in 1846. Extensive changes to the interior in 1877 involved pulling down the old vestry, re-shaping the roof, removing the gallery and adding a tower, but by 1912 the tower was crumbling. Not until 1973 was it demolished and the present tower and steeple built. The picturesque peg mill operated by the Baron family for generations was dismantled in 1902, when the oak peg, which could move the entire wooden structure into the eye of the wind, wore out. Duck Street near Arthur's Lane owed its name to a large marl pit used for brickmaking. Emptied of its clay, the hollow filled up with water and soon became a haven for ducks. It was drained in the mid-19th century and now has not a duck in sight. Duck Street is but one example of past history, as is Peg's Pool, Hambleton, which was near the Peg Mill.

The Creek, Hambleton, 1963. Last century this was where the wagonettes drew up for passengers to alight and sample the celebrated 'Hambleton Hookings', a particularly fine type of mussel caught with an iron hook. Sometimes they contained a pearl.

Printed from a glass negative dating from about 1880, this is thought to be Oddlands Cottage, Moss Side, Hambleton. In 1888 James and Elizabeth Acton lived here. Elizabeth, who was famed throughout Lancashire for her excellent butter, also made toffee and nettle beer to sell to tourists.

Rural Hambleton at the turn of the century was indeed quiet, but villagers had seen Blackpool Tower rise and were keen to sample 'the Wonderland of the World'. In 1896 they organised a trip and occupied one of the 30 large carriages on the Big Wheel. Pilgrims of Elswick started a bus service early in the 20th century.

At the opening of Shard Bridge in September 1864 a procession of landaus, wagonettes and carts passed over. The River Wyre was running high on this celebratory occasion. In the 17th century the Parke family farmed land alongside the river. They were ferrymen, and by the 18th century had built Ferry House, a site later occupied by Shard Bridge Inn.

Thomas Shorrock at Shorrocks Farm, Wharles, once known as Wharles Hall Farm, *c.* 1898. Traction engines and threshing machines were kept in the stack yard here. Isaac Ball and Son Ltd, 'wood roller trackers and threshing machine proprietors' at Wharles, served over 50 farms. Among Isaac's workmen were Thomas Ball, who lived at Laburnum Cottage and Henry S. Ward at Rhododendron Cottage. Three villages, Treales, Wharles and Roseacre (pronounced locally Trayls, Warls and Rozaker) were so close as to seem indivisible, a group of thatched cottages and farms. In Barrett's Directory of 1926, 46 farmers are listed.

Singleton Church, 1971. At the left side of the church door are two ancient stone sockets of the type found at the base of boundary crosses, which centuries ago were placed at strategic points to mark the limits of a parish. The old custom of 'beating or riding the bounds' impressed upon people's minds the importance of remembering the extent of boundaries, so young people always accompanied the annual walking party and were usually rewarded.

This heavy road roller from last century was one of those driven by 'Old Jem' (Jemmy Barron) and owned by Isaac Ball. The heavy rollers and traction engines for tar-spraying, road-making and harvesting were hired out by farmers and urban district councils.

Thatcher John Burke is at work in Market Street, Hambleton, 12 September 1964. Oat straw was not suitable for thatching so he is using Norfolk reeds. A steady trade in the Fylde last century, the art is dying out as there is now little demand.

Cottage at Crossmoor, Elswick, from an 1880s glass negative. Elswick and Larbreck were part of the ecclesiastical district with Great Eccleston in the 1920s when the church of St Anne, erected 1723, was completely restored. Mr Hawthornthwaite of Bombay presented a three-light window in memory of his father, a St Anne's-on-the-Sea vicar.

The old Pinfold at Crook Gate, Out Rawcliffe, 1880s. Straying sheep and cattle were confined here until their owners claimed them. Pound Fold and Pond Fold at Crossmoor are names which could have their origin in Pinfold, as every village had one.

The Old Hall, Winmarleigh, home of John Ball JP, *c.* 1912. Note the 'moss stocks' by the wall. These were petrified roots of trees hundreds of years old discovered during the draining of the mosslands, having been preserved to a remarkable toughness by the bog. Some villagers made carvings from them.

Weeton post office, seen here in the 1900s, was housed in a typical thatched Fylde cottage with large chimneys at the gable ends and a solitary telegraph pole to underline its status. As years went by, thatch was often covered with corrugated iron to keep out the rain.

Preesall, *c.* 1890. The whitewashed round house, later called Rose Cottage, was once a toll house in the days of the Turnpike Trusts, where coaches stopped on the way to Lancaster. On the far right is the village general store, and nearby the Saracen's Head Inn, which was featured in a novel *Death Drops the Pilot* by G. Bellairs.

Preesall Mill was built in 1839, and photographed in about 1911. To reach this six-storey windmill wagonettes and charabancs rattled over Shard Bridge, where tolls were payable. A brick tower mill, it was one of the two tallest windmills in the Fylde. Each sail was 38 ft long and there was a platform encircling the tower. The ground floor held sacks of corn; the second storey was the office where Mr Bisbrown, the miller, kept his books of accounts; the third storey housed bins into which the flour poured as it was ground by the millstones. Above that was the machinery: the huge, horizontal wheel that turned the millstones, the revolving shaft, and the flywheel. James Bisbrown, who was miller in 1866, was one of the family connected with Preesall Mill for generations.

# Acknowledgements

I am indebted to the late Harry Hodgkinson of London for passing on to me research into his family who lived around Poulton, and whose family tree he traced back as far as 1585.

Thanks are also due to the following:

Charles Ashton • Elsie Ayrton • Miss S. Ballard • *Blackpool Gazette*
Mr J.H. Bowers • Mr and Mrs W. Brown • Alison Callum • Tony Coppin
Alderman Jack Davies • Bob Gibson• Mrs N. Gibson
Chris and Helen Gleave • Harry Gleave • Derek Hawthornthwaite
Hodgson High School • Mr J.P. Innes • Pat James • David Jones • Ernie Kay
Lancashire Library • Lancashire Record Office • Mr and Mrs R. Poole
Poulton C. of E. School • Ron Severs • Ian Spencer • Harry Steer
*Thornton-Cleveleys Gazette* • Jim Ward • Mr W.M. Watson
Revd Colin Williams • Windsor Woollies • Cyril and Nora Wroe • Bill Yates

# BRITAIN IN OLD PHOTOGRAPHS

To order any of these titles please telephone Littlehampton Book Services on 01903 721596